GE-RE-D

Crash Bang Zoom

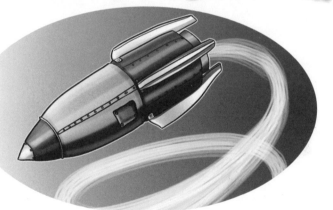

by PHiL Kettle

ILLUStrated by
Melissa Webb

Get Real
Crash Bang Zoom

Written by Phil Kettle
Illustrations by Melissa Webb
Character design by David Dunstan

Published by
Macmillan Education Australia Pty Ltd
Level 1, 15–19 Claremont Street, South Yarra,
Victoria 3141
www.macmillan.com.au

Edited by Emma Short

Designed by Jenny Lindstedt,
Goanna Graphics (Vic) Pty Ltd

Printed in China
10 9 8 7 6 5 4 3 2 1

ISBN: (pack) 9781420291094

ISBN: 9781420290868

Contents

Introduction

Say hello to Harry Harvard and Jesse Harrison. The one on the right with his fingers in his ears is Jesse. The one on the left with his fingers in his ears is Harry. The one standing in the middle, who looks like he is in a really cranky mood, is Principal Dorking.

You might be wondering why Jesse and Harry have their fingers in their ears, and why Principal Dorking is looking cranky. Well, I know why, and if you want to know why, then you'll just have to keep reading the rest of this non-fiction story.

(And if you really believe that this is a non-fiction story, then you probably believe that once upon a time, a cow really did jump over the moon...)

Chapter One

A Great and Wonderful Idea

Talented
Science Teacher
at work
DO NOT DISTURB

This story begins on the morning of a
very long day at Average Primary School.
Jesse and Harry were sitting in the science
laboratory with the rest of Mrs Payne's
Grade Six students. They were totally
engrossed in what their science teacher,
Mr Zimmer, was telling them.

A NOTE FROM THE AUTHOR

I suggest that you should be sitting or lying down when you read this very nearly true story. If you're not sitting or lying down, then you must be standing. And if you're standing, you should be prepared to fall to the ground in uncontrollable fits of laughter. So I hope you're standing on top of a mattress so you won't hurt yourself when you fall.

I wrote this story standing on the beach. So when I fell down in uncontrollable fits of laughter, I fell onto the soft sand. It didn't hurt one little bit!

And now get ready for a very long sentence!

Somewhere between Mr Zimmer trying
to explain how to get a rocket into orbit
and what would happen when that
rocket returned to Earth, Jesse came up
with another great and wonderful idea.

"Hey!" Jesse whispered in Harry's ear. "I think I've come up with another great and wonderful idea!"

"I hope it's great and wonderful and something to do with getting out of this boring class," Harry whispered back. "Maybe it will inspire us to do something hilariously funny?"

"I think it will," Jesse nodded, and this is how he described his great and wonderful idea.

1. **G**rab the remote control for the time machine from my backpack.

2. **P**ress the purple button to freeze time.

3. Race around the science laboratory and change all the labels on the chemical bottles.

4. Press the green button to re-start time.

5. Sit back, wait, and watch what happens when Mr Zimmer tries to mix a chemical formula.

"That's the same great and wonderful idea you always have during science class," said Harry.

"I know," said Jesse. "But it's so great and wonderful that it's worth having over and over again!"

Chapter Two

Get Ready for Take-off!

Mr Zimmer was always excited when he was teaching science. He was always extremely excited when he was talking about one of his favourite scientific subjects – space travel. Today he excitedly announced an exciting announcement to the class.

Today we are going to build a rocket that can travel to outer space!

A REMINDER FROM THE AUTHOR

For his whole life, Mr Zimmer has been working on special inventions that will make the world a better place. You might remember that recently, he went to a conference to work together with a team of very talented science teachers to create a unique chemical formula. This formula would be used to create his special invention – a spray that could vaporise problem students forever!

A moment earlier, all the Grade Six students had been struggling to stay awake. But now all the Grade Six students sat up straight and alert.

"Did you say we're going to build a rocket?" they all said at the same time.

"Yes," Mr Zimmer replied. "We're going to build a rocket and it's going to be the best rocket ever built at Average Primary School."

"It will probably be the only rocket ever built at Average Primary School," Harry whispered, winking at Jesse.

Chapter Three

A Bit of This, a Bit of That

The next thirty minutes were filled with the sounds of hammering, banging, nailing, chiselling, screw driving, gluing and shaping.

"Tools down!" shouted Mr Zimmer excitedly when thirty minutes were up.

The best-looking student-built rocket ever constructed now occupied the empty space at the front of the science laboratory.

All the Grade Six students stood back to admire their workmanship. They had to agree with Mr Zimmer. Their rocket really was the best-looking student-built rocket ever constructed.

"There's only one thing left to do," said Mr Zimmer excitedly.

"What's that?" asked Lenny 'the Stink' Edwards.

"We've got to launch the rocket, of course," Mr Zimmer continued. "But first, we're going to need some rocket fuel."

Mr Zimmer asked the students to collect all the chemical bottles in the science laboratory.

"We need to mix a bit of this with a bit of that, and a pinch of this with a handful of that," he said. "Then we'll stir it all together."

Mr Zimmer poured different amounts of the contents of the bottles into a test tube on the bench at the front of the science laboratory. "This is going to be the BEST rocket fuel ever," he finished.

Jesse and Harry looked sideways at each other. They winked and smiled and tried very hard, but not very successfully, to stifle their giggles.

Mr Zimmer poured the test tube full of the BEST rocket fuel ever into the best-looking student-built rocket ever constructed. Then he asked the entire class to follow him out of the science laboratory, down the corridor and towards the school oval. He also asked them to carry the best-looking student-built rocket ever constructed, which they did.

When they reached the middle of the oval, the Grade Six students gathered around the best-looking student-built rocket ever constructed.

"Students, I name this rocket the *Zimmer*," declared Mr Zimmer proudly.

Chapter four

KABOOM!

A moment later, Mr Zimmer pressed a button to launch the best-looking student-built rocket ever constructed on its way to outer space.

At first, the *Zimmer* flew straight up into the air until it was so high in the sky that the students had to squint to see it. But then…

The *Zimmer* disappeared in a cloud of smoke high in the sky above the oval.

"Where did it go?" said Mr Zimmer, starting to look worried.

Nobody said anything. Then Harry and Jesse gave up trying to stifle their giggles. They laughed and laughed and laughed.

"That sure was the BEST rocket fuel ever," said Jesse, when he finally stopped laughing.

"You're not wrong!" Harry agreed.

Mr Zimmer frowned. He had a very bad feeling about this whole situation.

Suddenly the rocket reappeared, very quickly, heading straight down towards the school canteen.

"RUN FOR YOUR LIVES!" called Mr Zimmer. The students took off as fast as they could go back towards the safety of the science laboratory.

Back in the science laboratory,
Mr Zimmer dropped to his knees and
thumped his fists on the floor.

"No, *no*, NO!" he wailed. "Why me?"

The rest of the Grade Six students
dropped to their knees and dissolved into
hysterical fits of laughter. But little did
they know that the adventure had only
just begun.

For everyone else in Average Primary
School, it was just another average day...

Average Stuff
in Average
Primary School

- Marge and Betty Large cooking up a storm

- Mrs Payne making students write lines

- Principal Dorking doing very little indeed

Not So Average Stuff in Average Primary School

- The best-looking student-built rocket ever constructed being launched from the middle of the Average Primary School oval and nobody noticing it

Chapter five

Five Minutes Earlier

A NOTE FROM THE AUTHOR

Five minutes earlier than it was when Mr Zimmer and the Grade Six students had gathered in the middle of the school oval to launch the best-looking student-built rocket ever constructed, this was what was happening in the school canteen...and I hope you're not out of breath after reading this sentence!

The canteen helpers, Betty and Marge Large, were having a very average day. They were cooking up a storm under the watchful eye of Mrs McBurger, the canteen manager.

Today's Menu

Something old, something new.

Today's special is stew, stew, stew.

(And hopefully it won't make you spew!)

In fact, Betty and Marge Large were so busy cooking up a storm that they didn't hear the giant 'kaboom' in the sky. And they didn't notice the *Zimmer* as it sped speedily and unstoppably towards the roof of the school canteen.

But of course, they both noticed the *Zimmer* when it crashed through the roof and smashed its way through the kitchen, destroying everything in its path. And they were very glad to see the back of it when it shot through the canteen window.

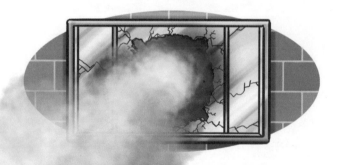

"Phew, that was close," said Betty Large, picking herself up off the floor.

"Yes, at least it missed the stew," replied Marge Large, with a sigh of relief.

Chapter Six

Worse to Come

Meanwhile, Mrs Payne was having
a very average day in her Grade Six
classroom. She was thinking of new
lines for naughty students to write while
she waited for her Grade Six students to
return from Mr Zimmer's science class.

In fact, Mrs Payne was thinking so hard that she didn't hear the giant 'kaboom' in the sky. And she didn't notice the *Zimmer* as it sped speedily and unstoppably towards the school canteen, smashed its way through the kitchen, and shot through the canteen window.

ANOTHER NOTE FROM THE AUTHOR

Sorry, that was another really long sentence. I hope you're not out of breath again! And here comes another one...

But she definitely noticed the *Zimmer* when it burst through her classroom window, circled around the classroom sending books and paper flying everywhere, whooshed out the classroom door, and continued on its route of destruction.

"My goodness me," said Mrs Payne. "What on Earth was that?"

Meanwhile, Principal Dorking was also having a very average day in his Average Primary School office. In fact, Principal Dorking was doing what all good school principals do – which was very little indeed.

PRINCIPAL GENIUS

Principal Dorking was so busy doing very little indeed that he didn't hear the giant 'kaboom' in the sky above the school oval. And he didn't notice the *Zimmer* as it sped speedily and unstoppably towards the school canteen, smashed its way through the kitchen, shot through the canteen window, burst through Mrs Payne's classroom window, circled around the classroom sending books and paper flying everywhere, and whooshed out the classroom door.

YET ANOTHER NOTE FROM THE AUTHOR

Oh dear, that was another really, really long sentence. If you're not out of breath, you might just be dead!

But of course, Principal Dorking definitely noticed the *Zimmer* when it whizzed through the corridor outside his office, swung sharply around the corner, bounced across his desk causing complete chaos, slammed through the office window, and disappeared into the distance.

41

Principal Dorking knew just what to do in an emergency. He picked up the phone and dialled 111111.

A REMINDER FROM THE AUTHOR

If you've read another book in this series, *The Flying Machines*, you'll know that this is the local Average phone number for EXTREME emergencies. It must only be dialled in an EXTREME emergency!

"Operator, please connect me to Captain Crash at Average Air Force. This is an EXTREME emergency!" said Principal Dorking.

"Putting you through, sir," came the reply.

Principal Dorking explained the situation to Captain Crash. Meanwhile, chaos reigned supreme at Average Primary School and the *Zimmer* continued on its merry way.

A QUESTION FROM THE AUTHOR

What is chaos?

AN ANSWER FROM THE AUTHOR

A dog chasing a cat in a china shop!

The *Zimmer* zigged and zagged and dashed and darted all around the school, terrifying students and teachers, and wrecking nearly everything in its path.

Captain Crash promised to get there as soon as he could.

Chapter Seven

Smash and Crash

Principal Dorking rushed outside and saw what was left of the school canteen.

"Oh no!" he yelled. "My lunch is going to be totally ruined!"

Mr Zimmer rushed outside and decided it was all too much. He kept rushing all the way to the car park, got in his car and drove home.

Mrs Payne rushed outside, surveyed the situation and thought hard. At first she thought that maybe the world was coming to an end. But suddenly another thought sprang into her mind.

"Hmmm," she said to Principal Dorking. "Where there's smoke…"

"There's fire!" finished Principal Dorking. "You're right, Mrs Payne. I've already called Captain Crash of the Average Air Force, but I'd better call the fire department too."

"No," said Mrs Payne. "I mean where there's smoke there's…JESSE HARRISON AND HARRY HARVARD!"

A NOTE FROM THE AUTHOR

That was a really short chapter, to make up for all those long sentences in the last chapter!

Chapter eight

What Happened Next

The Lord Mayor was snoozing on the steps of the Average Town Hall. Suddenly he heard a ZOOOOOOM overhead and woke up with a start.

"If I'm not mistaken, that's Captain Crash!" he said to himself.

The Lord Mayor grabbed the nearest megaphone and did what all good lord mayors do. He made a speech. "Average citizens," he announced. "Average is under attack. I will do everything I can to help and protect you."

Faster than a rat being chased by a very hungry rat-catching cat, he ran to his office and hid under his desk.

Scoop Jones was sitting at his desk enjoying a cup of hot chocolate when he heard the Lord Mayor's announcement. He grabbed his note pad and pencil, jumped on his trusty tricycle, and headed for Average Primary School.

A NOTE FROM THE AUTHOR

Scoop Jones used to ride a bicycle, but he kept falling off.

"I know from past experience that if there's trouble in Average, it always seems to come from Average Primary School," he told anyone who would listen along the way.

Constable Chris Cross from the Average police noticed Scoop Jones riding his tricycle down the street. Without a moment's hesitation, he ran out of the police station and followed Scoop Jones down the street towards Average Primary School. Constable Chris Cross blew his whistle very loudly the whole way. He really hoped that by the end of the day, he might have arrested someone and locked that someone in jail, because that was his very favourite thing to do.

When Scoop Jones and Constable Chris Cross reached Average Primary School, Captain Crash was flying his plane in circles over the school oval. The *Zimmer* was still zooming around, smashing and bashing everything in its path. Mrs Payne and Principal Dorking were ducking and weaving as it flew over their heads. And Harry and Jesse had climbed up onto the roof of the school library to watch the fun.

"Oh no," said Harry. "Principal Dorking must have called Captain Crash from the Average Air Force. The *Zimmer* could be in big trouble!"

"Don't worry," said Jesse. "Don't you remember what happened the last time Principal Dorking called Captain Crash?"

"Oh yes," Harry replied. "I think I do..."

Suddenly the *Zimmer* started flying in circles around Captain Crash's plane. Captain Crash started flying in circles around the *Zimmer*. The circles got smaller and smaller and smaller until...

The *Zimmer* shot straight up into the air, heading for outer space. Captain Crash's plane headed straight back down to the ground.

"I guess that's the end of the *Zimmer*," said Harry.

"And it looks like the end of Captain Crash...again!" said Jesse.

Chapter Nine

At the End of the Day

Captain Crash's parachute landed in the middle of the oval. Constable Chris Cross helped him to his feet and Scoop Jones took plenty of notes. There was a lot of shaking of heads and hands. Then Captain Crash, Constable Chris Cross and Scoop Jones headed back to town, leaving Principal Dorking and Mrs Payne alone in the middle of the oval.

"Hey Jesse, Principal Dorking is looking our way," said Harry, still perched on top of the school library.

"And Harry, he doesn't look very happy," said Jesse, still perched next to Harry.

Principal Dorking and Mrs Payne started walking quickly towards the library. Mrs Payne was frowning more than usual and Principal Dorking was shaking his fists.

"Do you think we should use the time machine to take us back to this morning?" asked Jesse. "Before we changed all the labels on the chemical bottles in the science laboratory."

"Yes, I think that might be yet another great and wonderful idea!" said Harry.

60

Chapter Ten

The Next Day

The next day was just another average day at Average Primary School. Marge and Betty Large were cooking up a storm, Mrs Payne was making Jesse and Harry write lines, and Principal Dorking was sitting in his office doing very little indeed.

But far away in outer space…

The
End

63

Let's Write

I always get excited when I'm about to write another story. First I get an idea, then I make a plan including location and characters. When my plan is finished, I'm ready to start my writing adventure.

If you've already read the first series of *Get Real*, and I think you probably have, then you might remember that writing a story is an adventure into your own imagination. The best thing about writing is that you take yourself into another world, where you are TOTALLY in charge. A writing adventure is a lot like a real-life adventure – there are some things that happen in a real-life adventure that you never planned to happen! So when you start your writing adventure, there will be some ideas that you plan and others that will just pop into your head!

Now turn back to page 5 of this story and read the introduction again.

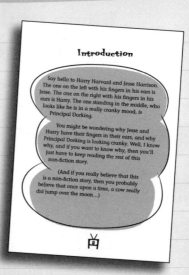

Now turn back to page 5 of this story and read the introduction again.

Why don't you use the introduction from this story to write your very own story about Jesse and Harry? You can take a writing adventure where you are TOTALLY in charge. There might be some things that you plan to happen, and there might be some things that you don't plan to happen. But remember, that's all part of the adventure into your own imagination. Enjoy!

Jesse and Harry Present

About the Author

Jesse: Hey Phil, have you ever built a rocket?

Phil: No, why do you ask?

Jesse: I want to know where you got the idea for this story.

Phil: Well, I've never built a rocket but once I built the best-looking billy cart in the world.

Jesse: What happened to it?

Phil: I took it up to the top of a hill then drove it so fast down the hill I felt like I was in a rocket.

Jesse: How did you stop it?

Phil: I didn't. A really big tree did.

About the Illustrator

Harry: Hey Melissa, have you ever been in a rocket?

Melissa: Not yet!

Harry: Well, you sure are good at drawing one!

Melissa: Thank you!

Word-up!

Argument: a discussion that you have when you're right

Clothes dryer: an appliance designed to eat socks

Save me!

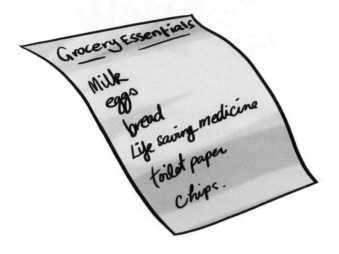

Grocery list: something that your mother or father spends an hour writing and then forgets to take to the supermarket

Diet soda: a drink you buy to wash down a bar of chocolate

Eternity: the last minute of a close football game

A Laugh a Minute!

Why was the number six scared of the number seven?
He had heard people say that seven ate nine!

How does the abominable snowman get to the shop?
By icicle!

What do you call a fly without wings?
A walk!

What is the best thing to put into a cake?
Your teeth!

What do you get if you cross the Atlantic with the Titanic?
About halfway!

Other Titles in the

Series